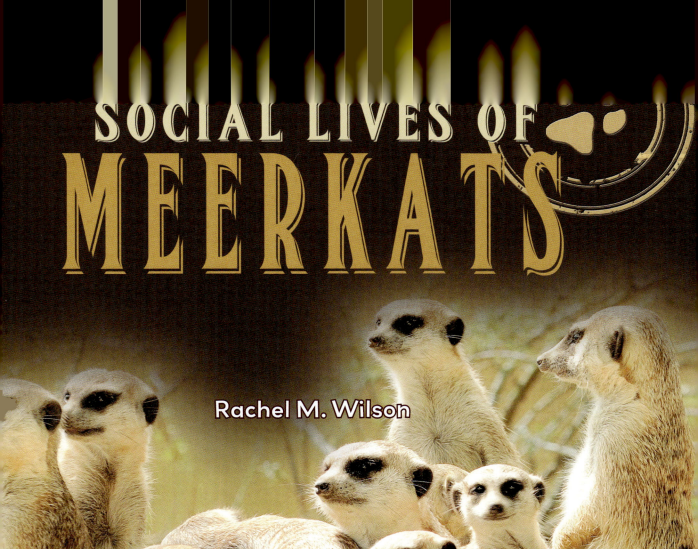

# SOCIAL LIVES OF
# MEERKATS

Rachel M. Wilson

**Rourke**
Educational Media

rourkeeducationalmedia.com

Scan for Related Titles
and Teacher Resources

## Teaching Focus:

Reading Comprehension: Use specific comprehension strategies, such as the use of story structure, to help students increase their reading comprehension.

## Before Reading:

### Building Academic Vocabulary and Background Knowledge

Before reading a book, it is important to set the stage for your child or student by using pre-reading strategies. This will help them develop their vocabulary, increase their reading comprehension, and make connections across the curriculum.

1. Read the title and look at the cover. *Let's make predictions about what this book will be about.*
2. Take a picture walk by talking about the pictures/photographs in the book. Implant the vocabulary as you take the picture walk. Be sure to talk about the text features such as headings, Table of Contents, glossary, bolded words, captions, charts/diagrams, and Index.
3. Have students read the first page of text with you then have students read the remaining text.
4. Strategy Talk – use to assist students while reading.
   - Get your mouth ready
   - Look at the picture
   - Think…does it make sense
   - Think…does it look right
   - Think…does it sound right
   - Chunk it – by looking for a part you know
5. Read it again.
6. After reading the book complete the activities below.

### Content Area Vocabulary
*Use glossary words in a sentence.*

aggression
bond
burrows
huddle
offspring
sacrifice

## After Reading:

### Comprehension and Extension Activity

After reading the book, work on the following questions with your child or students in order to check their level of reading comprehension and content mastery.

1. *What is the responsibility of the guard?* (Summarize)
2. *Name a type of food baby meerkats eat.* (Asking questions)
3. *When a meerkat shouts, what could it mean?* (Text to self connection)
4. *What do weaker or more submissive meerkats do to keep the dominant members happy?* (Summarize)

### Extension Activity

Make your own 3-D meerkat. You will need construction paper, poster board, colored pencils, glue, and scissors. Draw a meerkat on the construction paper using a picture from the book. Color it in. Glue your picture to the poster board to make it stronger. Cut it out. Glue the tail to the back of the poster board so it can stand on its own. Have your friends do the same and you can have fun with your meerkat family!

# TABLE OF CONTENTS

# SURVIVING TOGETHER

Meerkats groom and sunbathe each morning. They pick through each other's fur. They snack on the bugs they find. This helps meerkats relax and **bond**.

Together, they dig out safe **burrows.** They find insects and lizards to eat. And together, they care for their young.

Meerkats live in social groups of three to 50 on the dry plains of southern Africa. A group of meerkats is called a mob or a gang.

Adults take turns babysitting. They give up food to do this. Their **sacrifice** keeps the group healthy.

Baby meerkats beg for food. They fight for it too! Soon, they learn to feed themselves.

Would you give a scorpion to a baby? Adult meerkats remove stingers at first to teach babies about dangerous prey.

7

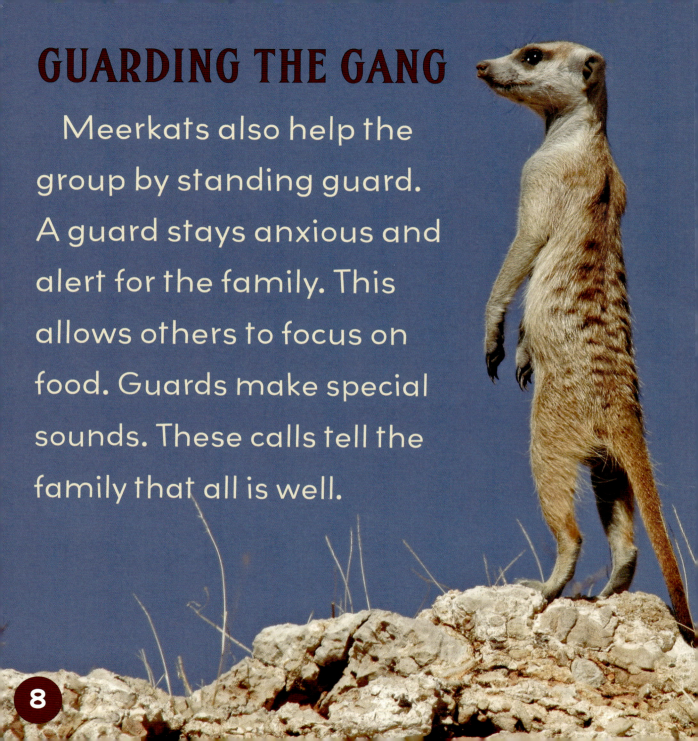

# GUARDING THE GANG

Meerkats also help the group by standing guard. A guard stays anxious and alert for the family. This allows others to focus on food. Guards make special sounds. These calls tell the family that all is well.

Fear makes young meerkats cry out. Older meerkats say more with their cries. They share the level of danger. They even tell whether a threat comes from above or below.

# AGGRESSION AND DOMINANCE

Still, meerkat families are not always peaceful. Meerkats fight over food and steal it.

A jealous meerkat may stop others from grooming.

Sometimes, meerkats challenge their group's leaders for control. More often, they leave to start or to join a new group.

One male and female in the group have most of the **offspring.** These dominant, or bossy, meerkats run the show.

A new mother turns fierce and aggressive. She may kick out other females. She may even kill their young. Weaker, or submissive, meerkats groom this female to keep her happy—and less violent.

Meerkats use **aggression** to show strength and power. Dominant meerkats can be bullies. They may bite or hit their victims. They chase, charge, or slam hips.

Fearful meerkats hide from attack. They make themselves small and cry out. Sadly, this will not help. The only way to avoid a meerkat attack is to avoid the bully.

When an enemy threatens, meerkats work together. Their best defense is called mobbing.

One meerkat growls. Then, the group forms a fierce mob. They stand tall and bob their heads. They raise their tails. Their hair stands on end.

# FUN TO WATCH

Meerkats do not mind being watched by scientists. One meerkat group even became famous for it.

Humans enjoyed watching meerkat drama on the TV show *Meerkat Manor.*

Meerkat guards seek out the highest point—they may *even* climb on a human scientist's head!

Meerkat nights end as their days begin. The group shares in grooming.

Then they **huddle** for warmth in the burrow, together, as always.

21

# PHOTO GLOSSARY

**aggression** (uh-GRESH-uhn): Aggression is behavior that threatens or attacks. Meerkat aggression includes biting, hitting, and chasing.

**bond** (bahnd): To bond is to come together. When social animals bond, they feel connected.

**burrows** (BUR-ohz): Burrows are connected tunnels and holes underground.

**huddle** (HUHD-uhl): To huddle is to gather close. Meerkats huddle in their burrows for safety and warmth.

**offspring** (AWF-spring): Offspring are the children of an animal.

**sacrifice** (SAK-ruh-fise): To sacrifice is to give something up for the good of another.

# Index

**Meet The Author!**
www.meetREMauthors.

# Websites to Visit

www.fellowearthlings.org/index.html
http://kids.nationalgeographic.com/animals/
   meerkat/#meerkat-group.jpg
http://animals.sandiegozoo.org/animals/meerkat

# About the Author

Rachel M. Wilson grew up in Alabama in a house full of animals. Rac
studied Theater at Northwestern University and Writing for Children
& Young Adults at Vermont College of Fine Arts. Her debut novel, *Don'*
*Touch*, was published in 2014. These days, Rachel writes, acts, and
teaches in Chicago, IL, where she shares a home with her best friend,
dog named Remy Frankenstein.

**Library of Congress PCN Data**

Social Lives of Meerkats / Rachel M. Wilson
(Animal Behaviors)
ISBN 978-1-68191-701-6 (hard cover)
ISBN 978-978-1-68191-802-0 (soft cover)
ISBN 978-1-68191-899-0 (e-Book)
Library of Congress Control Number: 2016932579

Rourke Educational Media
Printed in the United States of America, North Mankato, Minnesota

© 2017 Rourke Educational Media

www.rourkeeducationalmedia.com

Edited by: Keli Sipperley
Cover design, interior design and art direction: Nicola Stratford
www.nicolastratford.com

PHOTO CREDITS: Cover © Cover and title page © anetapics; pag
© nattanan726, page 5 top © Grobler du Preez, bottom © Aneta
page 6 © cathsmithdotcom, page 7 © tryptophanatic; page 8 © E
Print, page 9 © defpicture; page 10 © Pyshnyy Maxim Vjacheslav
page 11 © Jerry Sharp; page 12-13 © tratong; page 14 © Sokol
Alexey, page 15 © Tsepova Ekaterina; page 16-17 © EcoPrint; pe
18-19 © Jiri Haureljuk; Page 20-21 © Jacek Jasinski. All photos fr
Shutterstock.com

**Also Available as:**

24